D0705984

JOINT DECLARATION
ON THE
DOCTRINE OF JUSTIFICATION

JOINT DECLARATION
ON THE
DOCTRINE OF JUSTIFICATION

The Lutheran World Federation
and
The Roman Catholic Church

William B. Eerdmans Publishing Company
Grand Rapids, Michigan / Cambridge, U.K.

Originally published as
Gemeinsame Erklärung zur Rechtfertigungslehre
© 1999 Verlag Otto Lembeck, Frankfurt am Main;
Bonifatius-Verlag, Paderborn;
Lutherischer Weltbund;
Päpstlicher Rat zur Förderung der Einheit der Christen
Gesamtherstellung: Druckerei und Verlag Otto Lembeck
Frankfurt am Main und Butzbach

English translation © 2000 by Wm. B. Eerdmans Publishing Co.,
The Lutheran World Federation, and
The Pontifical Council for Promoting Christian Unity

Published 2000 by
Wm. B. Eerdmans Publishing Co.
255 Jefferson Ave. S.E., Grand Rapids, Michigan 49503 /
P.O. Box 163, Cambridge CB3 9PU U.K.
All rights reserved

Printed in the United States of America

05 04 03 02 01   7 6 5 4 3 2

Library of Congress Cataloging-in-Publication Data

Gemeinsame Erklärung zur Rechtfertigungslehre. English.
Joint Declaration on the Doctrine of Justification /
The Lutheran World Federation and the Roman Catholic Church
p.   cm.
Includes bibliographical references.
ISBN 0-8028-4774-9
1. Justification — Congresses.   I. Lutheran World Federation.
II. Catholic Church.   III. Title
BT764.2 .G4613   2000
234'.7 — dc21
00-028845

www.eerdmans.com

CONTENTS

5

PREFACE

With great joy the Roman Catholic Church and the Lutheran World Federation herewith present the official text of the *Joint Declaration on the Doctrine of Justification*.

The solemn confirmation of this *Joint Declaration* on 31 October 1999 in Augsburg, by means of the *Official Common Statement* with its *Annex*, represents an ecumenical event of historical significance.

We recommend these texts for careful study in seminaries and in parishes, and we encourage a thorough reading of them by individual Christians. We request that common and deepening ecumenical reflection be continued on the biblical message of justification and its meaning for the churches, for the life of individual persons, and for human society.

We thank God that the decades of dialogue have reached this result. We are confident that it represents a good basis for the continued rapprochement of the ecumenical partners and that it will also be of value within the wider ecumenical movement.

Edward Idris Cardinal Cassidy
President
The Pontifical Council
for Promoting Christian Unity

Bishop Christian Krause
President
The Lutheran World Federation

Bishop Walter Kasper
Secretary
The Pontifical Council
for Promoting Christian Unity

Reverend Dr. Ishmael Noko
General Secretary
The Lutheran World Federation

JOINT DECLARATION ON THE DOCTRINE OF JUSTIFICATION

by the
Lutheran World Federation
and the Roman Catholic Church

Preamble

1. The doctrine of justification was of central importance for the Lutheran Reformation of the sixteenth century. It was held to be the "first and chief article"[1] and at the same time the "ruler and judge over all other Christian doctrines."[2] The doctrine of justification was particularly asserted and defended in its Reformation shape and special valuation over against the Roman Catholic Church and theology of that time, which in turn asserted and defended a doctrine of justification of a different character. From the Reformation perspective, justification was the crux of all the disputes. Doctrinal condemnations were put forward both in the Lutheran Confessions[3] and by the Roman Catholic Church's Council of Trent. These condemnations are still valid today and thus have a church-dividing effect.

2. For the Lutheran tradition, the doctrine of justification has retained its special status. Consequently it has also from the beginning occupied an important place in the official Lutheran–Roman Catholic dialogue.

3. Special attention should be drawn to the following reports: "The Gospel and the Church" (1972)[4] and "Church and Justification" (1994)[5] by the Lutheran–Roman Catholic Joint

---

1. The Smalcald Articles, II,1; Book of Concord, 292.

2. "Rector et judex super omnia genera doctrinarum" — Weimar Edition of Luther's Works (WA), 39,I,205.

3. It should be noted that some Lutheran churches include only the Augsburg Confession and Luther's Small Catechism among their binding confessions. These texts contain no condemnations about justification in relation to the Roman Catholic Church.

4. Report of the Joint Lutheran–Roman Catholic Study Commission, published in *Growth in Agreement* (New York and Geneva, 1984), pp. 168-89.

5. Published by the Lutheran World Federation (Geneva, 1994).

Commission, "Justification by Faith" (1983)[6] of the Lutheran–
Roman Catholic dialogue in the United States and "The Condemnations of the Reformation Era: Do They Still Divide?"
(1986)[7] by the Ecumenical Working Group of Protestant and
Catholic theologians in Germany. Some of these dialogue reports have been officially received by the churches. An important example of such reception is the binding response of the
United Evangelical–Lutheran Church of Germany to the "Condemnations" study, made in 1994 at the highest possible level
of ecclesiastical recognition together with the other churches
of the Evangelical Church in Germany.[8]

4. In their discussion of the doctrine of justification, all
the dialogue reports as well as the responses show a high de-
gree of agreement in their approaches and conclusions. The
time has therefore come to take stock and to summarize the
results of the dialogues on justification so that our churches
may be informed about the overall results of this dialogue
with the necessary accuracy and brevity, and thereby be en-
abled to make binding decisions.

5. The present *Joint Declaration* has this intention:
namely, to show that on the basis of their dialogue the
subscribing Lutheran churches and the Roman Catholic
Church[9] are now able to articulate a common understanding

---

6. *Lutheran and Catholics in Dialogue*, VII (Minneapolis, 1985).

7. Minneapolis, 1990.

8. "Gemeinsame Stellungnahme der Arnoldshainer Konferenz, der
Vereinigten Kirche und des Deutschen Nationalkomitees des Lutherischen
Weltbundes zum Dokument 'Lehrverurteilungen — kirchentrennend?'"
Ökumenische Rundschau 44 (1995): 99-102. See also the position papers that
underlie this resolution, in *Lehrverurteilungen im Gespräch, Die ersten offi-
ziellen Stellungnahmen aus den evangelischen Kirchen in Deutschland* (Göttingen:
Vandenhoeck & Ruprecht, 1993).

9. The word "church" is used in this *Declaration* to reflect the self-

of our justification by God's grace through faith in Christ. It does not cover all that either church teaches about justification; it does encompass a consensus on basic truths of the doctrine of justification and shows that the remaining differences in its explication are no longer the occasion for doctrinal condemnations.

6. Our *Declaration* is not a new, independent presentation alongside the dialogue reports and documents to date, let alone a replacement of them. Rather, as the appendix of Sources shows, it makes repeated reference to them and their arguments.

7. Like the dialogues themselves, this *Joint Declaration* rests on the conviction that in overcoming the earlier controversial questions and doctrinal condemnations, the churches neither take the condemnations lightly nor do they disavow their own past. On the contrary, this *Declaration* is shaped by the conviction that in their respective histories our churches have come to new insights. Developments have taken place that not only make possible but also require the churches to examine the divisive questions and condemnations and see them in a new light.

1. Biblical Message of Justification

8. Our common way of listening to the word of God in Scripture has led to such new insights. Together we hear the gospel that "God so loved the world that he gave his only

---

understandings of the participating churches, without intending to resolve all the ecclesiological issues related to this term.

Son, so that everyone who believes in him may not perish but may have eternal life" (Jn 3:16). This good news is set forth in Holy Scripture in various ways. In the Old Testament we listen to God's word about human sinfulness (Ps 51:1-5; Dan 9:5f; Eccl/Qoh 8:9f; Ezra 9:6f) and human disobedience (Gen 3:1-19; Neh 9:16f, 26) as well as about God's "righteousness" (Isa 46:13; 51:5-8; 56:1 [cf. 53:11]; Jer 9:24) and "judgment" (Eccl/Qoh 12:14; Ps 9:5f; 76:7-9).

9. In the New Testament diverse treatments of "righteousness" and "justification" are found in the writings of Matthew (5:10; 6:33; 21:32), John (16:8-11), Hebrews (5:3; 10:37f), and James (2:14-26).[10] In Paul's letters also, the gift of salvation is described in various ways: "for freedom Christ has set us free" (Gal 5:1-13; cf. Rom 6:7), "reconciled to God" (2 Cor 5:18-21; cf. Rom 5:11), "peace with God" (Rom 5:1), "new creation" (2 Cor 5:17), "alive to God in Christ Jesus" (Rom 6:11, 23), and "sanctified in Christ Jesus" (cf. 1 Cor 1:2, 30; 2 Cor 1:1). Chief among these is the "justification" of sinful human beings by God's grace through faith (Rom 3:23-25), which came into particular prominence in the Reformation period.

10. Paul sets forth the gospel as the power of God for salvation of the person who has fallen under the power of sin, as the message that proclaims that "the righteousness of God is revealed through faith for faith" (Rom 1:16f) and that

---

10. Cf. "Malta Report," paras. 26-30; "Justification by Faith," paras. 122-47. At the request of the US dialogue on justification, the non-Pauline New Testament texts were addressed in *Righteousness in the New Testament*, by John Reumann, with responses by Joseph A. Fitzmyer and Jerome D. Quinn (Philadelphia and New York, 1982), pp. 124-80. The results of this study were summarized in the dialogue report "Justification by Faith" in paras. 139-42.

grants "justification" (Rom 3:21-31). He proclaims Christ as "our righteousness" (1 Cor 1:30), applying to the risen Lord what Jeremiah proclaimed about God himself (Jer 23:6). In Christ's death and resurrection all dimensions of his saving work have their roots, for he is "our Lord, who was put to death for our trespasses and raised for our justification" (Rom 4:25). All human beings are in need of God's righteousness, "since all have sinned and fall short of the glory of God" (Rom 3:23; cf. Rom 1:18–3:20; 11:32; Gal 3:22). In Galatians (3:6) and Romans (4:3-9), Paul understands Abraham's faith (Gen 15:6) as faith in the God who justifies the sinner (Rom 4:5) and calls upon the testimony of the Old Testament to undergird his gospel that this righteousness will be reckoned to all who, like Abraham, trust in God's promise. "For the righteous will live by faith" (Hab 2:4; cf. Gal 3:11; Rom 1:17). In Paul's letters, God's righteousness is also God's power for those who have faith (Rom 1:16f; 2 Cor 5:21). In Christ he makes it our righteousness (2 Cor 5:21). Justification becomes ours through Christ Jesus, "whom God put forward as a sacrifice of atonement by his blood, effective through faith" (Rom 3:25; see 3:21-28). "For by grace you have been saved through faith, and this is not your own doing; it is the gift of God — not the result of works" (Eph 2:8f).

11. Justification is the forgiveness of sins (cf. Rom 3:23-25; Acts 13:39; Lk 18:14), liberation from the dominating power of sin and death (Rom 5:12-21) and from the curse of the law (Gal 3:10-14). It is acceptance into communion with God — already now, but then fully in God's coming kingdom (Rom 5:1f). It unites with Christ and with his death and resurrection (Rom 6:5). It occurs in the reception of the Holy Spirit in baptism and incorporation into the one body (Rom

8:1f, 9f; 1 Cor 12:12f). All this is from God alone, for Christ's sake, by grace, through faith in "the gospel of God's Son" (Rom 1:1-3).

12. The justified live by faith that comes from the Word of Christ (Rom 10:17) and is active through love (Gal 5:6), the fruit of the Spirit (Gal 5:22f). But since the justified are assailed from within and without by powers and desires (Rom 8:35-39; Gal 5:16-21) and fall into sin (1 Jn 1:8, 10), they must constantly hear God's promises anew, confess their sins (1 Jn 1:9), participate in Christ's body and blood, and be exhorted to live righteously in accord with the will of God. That is why the Apostle says to the justified: "Work out your own salvation with fear and trembling; for it is God who is at work in you, enabling you both to will and to work for his good pleasure" (Phil 2:12f). But the good news remains: "there is now no condemnation for those who are in Christ Jesus" (Rom 8:1), and in whom Christ lives (Gal 2:20). Christ's "act of righteousness leads to justification and life for all" (Rom 5:18).

2. The Doctrine of Justification as Ecumenical Problem

13. Opposing interpretations and applications of the biblical message of justification were a principal cause of the division of the Western church in the sixteenth century and led as well to doctrinal condemnations. A common understanding of justification is therefore fundamental and indispensable to overcoming that division. By appropriating insights of recent biblical studies and drawing on modern

investigations of the history of theology and dogma, the post–Vatican II ecumenical dialogue has led to a notable convergence concerning justification, with the result that this *Joint Declaration* is able to formulate a consensus on basic truths concerning the doctrine of justification. In light of this consensus, the corresponding doctrinal condemnations of the sixteenth century do not apply to today's partner.

3. The Common Understanding of Justification

14. The Lutheran churches and the Roman Catholic Church have together listened to the good news proclaimed in Holy Scripture. This common listening, together with the theological conversations of recent years, has led to a shared understanding of justification. This encompasses a consensus in the basic truths; the differing explications in particular statements are compatible with it.

15. In faith we together hold the conviction that justification is the work of the triune God. The Father sent his Son into the world to save sinners. The foundation and presupposition of justification is the incarnation, death, and resurrection of Christ. Justification thus means that Christ himself is our righteousness, in which we share through the Holy Spirit in accord with the will of the Father. Together we confess: By grace alone, in faith in Christ's saving work and not because of any merit on our part, we are accepted by God and receive the Holy Spirit, who renews our hearts while equipping and calling us to good works.[11]

---

11. "All under One Christ," para. 14, in *Growth in Agreement*, 241-47.

16. All people are called by God to salvation in Christ. Through Christ alone are we justified, when we receive this salvation in faith. Faith is itself God's gift through the Holy Spirit, who works through Word and Sacrament in the community of believers and who, at the same time, leads believers into that renewal of life which God will bring to completion in eternal life.

17. We also share the conviction that the message of justification directs us in a special way toward the heart of the New Testament witness to God's saving action in Christ: it tells us that because we are sinners our new life is solely due to the forgiving and renewing mercy that God imparts as a gift and we receive in faith, and never can merit in any way.

18. Therefore the doctrine of justification, which takes up this message and explicates it, is more than just one part of Christian doctrine. It stands in an essential relation to all truths of faith, which are to be seen as internally related to each other. It is an indispensable criterion that constantly serves to orient all the teaching and practice of our churches to Christ. When Lutherans emphasize the unique significance of this criterion, they do not deny the interrelation and significance of all truths of faith. When Catholics see themselves as bound by several criteria, they do not deny the special function of the message of justification. Lutherans and Catholics share the goal of confessing Christ in all things, who alone is to be trusted above all things as the one Mediator (1 Tim 2:5f) through whom God in the Holy Spirit gives himself and pours out his renewing gifts. (See Sources for section 3.)

4. Explicating the Common Understanding of Justification

4.1. Human Powerlessness and Sin in Relation to Justification

19. We confess together that all persons depend completely on the saving grace of God for their salvation. The freedom they possess in relation to persons and the things of this world is no freedom in relation to salvation, for as sinners they stand under God's judgment and are incapable of turning by themselves to God to seek deliverance, of meriting their justification before God, or of attaining salvation by their own abilities. Justification takes place solely by God's grace. Because Catholics and Lutherans confess this together, it is true that:

20. When Catholics say that persons "cooperate" in preparing for and accepting justification by consenting to God's justifying action, they see such personal consent as itself an effect of grace, not as an action arising from innate human abilities.

21. According to Lutheran teaching, human beings are incapable of cooperating in their salvation because as sinners they actively oppose God and his saving action. Lutherans do not deny that a person can reject the working of grace. When they emphasize that a person can only receive (mere passive) justification, they mean thereby to exclude any possibility of contributing to one's own justification, but do not deny that believers are fully involved personally in their faith, which is effected by God's Word. (See Sources for 4.1.)

4.2. Justification as Forgiveness of Sins and Making Righteous

22. We confess together that God forgives sin by grace and at the same time frees human beings from sin's enslaving power and imparts the gift of new life in Christ. When persons come by faith to share in Christ, God no longer imputes to them their sin and through the Holy Spirit effects in them an active love. These two aspects of God's gracious action are not to be separated, for persons are by faith united with Christ, who in his person is our righteousness (1 Cor 1:30): both the forgiveness of sin and the saving presence of God himself. Because Catholics and Lutherans confess this together, it is true to say that:

23. When Lutherans emphasize that the righteousness of Christ is our righteousness, their intention is above all to insist that the sinner is granted righteousness before God in Christ through the declaration of forgiveness and that only in union with Christ is one's life renewed. When they stress that God's grace is forgiving love ("the favor of God"),[12] they do not thereby deny the renewal of the Christian's life. They intend rather to express that justification remains free from human cooperation and is not dependent on the life-renewing effects of grace in human beings.

24. When Catholics emphasize the renewal of the interior person through the reception of grace imparted as a gift to the believer,[13] they wish to insist that God's forgiving grace always brings with it a gift of new life, which in the

---

12. Cf. WA 8:106; American Edition 32:227.
13. Cf. Denzinger-Schönmetzer, *Enchiridion symbolorum* . . . (hereafter DS) 1528.

Holy Spirit becomes effective in active love. They do not thereby deny that God's gift of grace in justification remains independent of human cooperation. (See Sources for section 4.2.)

4.3. *Justification by Faith and through Grace*

25. We confess together that sinners are justified by faith in the saving action of God in Christ. By the action of the Holy Spirit in baptism, they are granted the gift of salvation, which lays the basis for the whole Christian life. They place their trust in God's gracious promise by justifying faith, which includes hope in God and love for him. Such a faith is active in love, and thus the Christian cannot and should not remain without works. But whatever in the justified precedes or follows the free gift of faith is neither the basis of justification nor merits it.

26. According to Lutheran understanding, God justifies sinners in faith alone (*sola fide*). In faith they place their trust wholly in their Creator and Redeemer and thus live in communion with him. God himself effects faith as he brings forth such trust by his creative word. Because God's act is a new creation, it affects all dimensions of the person and leads to a life in hope and love. In the doctrine of "justification by faith alone," a distinction but not a separation is made between justification itself and the renewal of one's way of life that necessarily follows from justification and without which faith does not exist. Thereby the basis is indicated from which the renewal of life proceeds, for it comes forth from the love of God imparted to the person in justification. Justification and renewal are joined in Christ, who is present in faith.

27. The Catholic understanding also sees faith as fundamental in justification. For without faith, no justification can take place. Persons are justified through baptism as hearers of the word and believers in it. The justification of sinners is forgiveness of sins and being made righteous by justifying grace, which makes us children of God. In justification the righteous receive from Christ faith, hope, and love and are thereby taken into communion with him.[14] This new personal relation to God is grounded totally in God's graciousness and remains constantly dependent on the salvific and creative working of this gracious God, who remains true to himself, so that one can rely upon him. Thus justifying grace never becomes a human possession to which one could appeal over against God. While Catholic teaching emphasizes the renewal of life by justifying grace, this renewal in faith, hope, and love is always dependent on God's unfathomable grace and contributes nothing to justification about which one could boast before God (Rom 3:27). (See Sources for section 4.3.)

4.4. The Justified as Sinner

28. We confess together that in baptism the Holy Spirit unites one with Christ, justifies, and truly renews the person. But the justified must all through life constantly look to God's unconditional justifying grace. They also are continuously exposed to the power of sin still pressing its attacks (cf. Rom 6:12-14) and are not exempt from a lifelong struggle against the contradiction to God within the selfish desires of

---

14. Cf. DS 1530.

the old Adam (see Gal 5:16; Rom 7:7-10). The justified also must ask God daily for forgiveness, as in the Lord's Prayer (Mt. 6:12; 1 Jn 1:9), are ever again called to conversion and penance, and are ever again granted forgiveness.

29. Lutherans understand this condition of the Christian as being "at the same time righteous and sinner." Believers are totally righteous, in that God forgives their sins through Word and Sacrament and grants the righteousness of Christ, which they appropriate in faith. In Christ, they are made just before God. Looking at themselves through the law, however, they recognize that they remain also totally sinners. Sin still lives in them (1 Jn 1:8; Rom 7:17, 20), for they repeatedly turn to false gods and do not love God with that undivided love which God requires as their Creator (Deut 6:5; Mt 22:36-40 par.). This contradiction to God is as such truly sin. Nevertheless, the enslaving power of sin is broken on the basis of the merit of Christ. It no longer is a sin that "rules" the Christian, for it is itself "ruled" by Christ with whom the justified are bound in faith. In this life, then, Christians can in part lead a just life. Despite sin, the Christian is no longer separated from God because in the daily return to baptism the person who has been born anew by baptism and the Holy Spirit has this sin forgiven. Thus this sin no longer brings damnation and eternal death.[15] Thus, when Lutherans say that justified persons are also sinners and that their opposition to God is truly sin, they do not deny that, despite this sin, they are not separated from God and that this sin is a "ruled" sin. In these affirmations, they are in agreement with Roman Catholics, despite the difference in understanding sin in the justified.

---

15. Cf. Apology II, 38-45; Book of Concord, 105f.

30. Catholics hold that the grace of Jesus Christ imparted in baptism takes away all that is sin "in the proper sense" and that is "worthy of damnation" (Rom 8:1).[16] There does, however, remain in the person an inclination (concupiscence) that comes from sin and presses toward sin. Since, according to Catholic conviction, human sins always involve a personal element and since this element is lacking in this inclination, Catholics do not see this inclination as sin in an authentic sense. They do not thereby deny that this inclination does not correspond to God's original design for humanity and that it is objectively in contradiction to God and remains one's enemy in lifelong struggle. Grateful for deliverance by Christ, they underscore that this inclination in contradiction to God does not merit the punishment of eternal death[17] and does not separate the justified person from God. But when individuals voluntarily separate themselves from God, it is not enough to return to observing the commandments, for they must receive pardon and peace in the Sacrament of Reconciliation through the word of forgiveness imparted to them in virtue of God's reconciling work in Christ. (See Sources for section 4.4.)

4.5. Law and Gospel

31. We confess together that persons are justified by faith in the gospel "apart from works prescribed by the law" (Rom 3:28). Christ has fulfilled the law and by his death and resurrection has overcome it as a way to salvation. We also

---

16. Cf. DS 1515.
17. Cf. DS 1515.

confess that God's commandments retain their validity for the justified and that Christ has by his teaching and example expressed God's will, which is a standard for the conduct of the justified also.

32. Lutherans state that the distinction and right ordering of law and gospel are essential for the understanding of justification. In its theological use, the law is demand and accusation. Throughout their lives, all persons, Christians also, in that they are sinners, stand under this accusation which uncovers their sin so that, in faith in the gospel, they will turn unreservedly to the mercy of God in Christ, which alone justifies them.

33. Because the law as a way to salvation has been fulfilled and overcome through the gospel, Catholics can say that Christ is not a lawgiver in the manner of Moses. When Catholics emphasize that the righteous are bound to observe God's commandments, they do not thereby deny that through Jesus Christ God has mercifully promised to his children the grace of eternal life.[18] (See Sources for section 4.5.)

4.6. *Assurance of Salvation*

34. We confess together that the faithful can rely on the mercy and promises of God. In spite of their own weakness and the manifold threats to their faith, on the strength of Christ's death and resurrection they can build on the effective promise of God's grace in Word and Sacrament and so be sure of this grace.

---

18. Cf. DS 1545.

35. This was emphasized in a particular way by the Reformers: in the midst of temptation, believers should not look to themselves but look solely to Christ and trust only him. In trust in God's promise they are assured of their salvation, but are never secure looking at themselves.

36. Catholics can share the concern of the Reformers to ground faith in the objective reality of Christ's promise, to look away from one's own experience, and to trust in Christ's forgiving word alone (cf. Mt 16:19; 18:18). With the Second Vatican Council, Catholics state: to have faith is to entrust oneself totally to God,[19] who liberates us from the darkness of sin and death and awakens us to eternal life.[20] In this sense, one cannot believe in God and at the same time consider the divine promise untrustworthy. No one may doubt God's mercy and Christ's merit. Every person, however, may be concerned about his salvation when he looks upon his own weaknesses and shortcomings. Recognizing his own failures, however, the believer may yet be certain that God intends his salvation. (See Sources for section 4.6.)

4.7. The Good Works of the Justified

37. We confess together that good works — a Christian life lived in faith, hope, and love — follow justification and are its fruits. When the justified live in Christ and act in the grace they receive, they bring forth, in biblical terms, good fruit. Since Christians struggle against sin their entire lives, this consequence of justification is also an obligation they

---

19. Cf. *Dei Verbum* (Vatican II) (hereafter *DV*) 5.
20. Cf. *DV* 5.

must fulfill. Thus both Jesus and the apostolic Scriptures admonish Christians to bring forth the works of love.

38. According to Catholic understanding, good works, made possible by grace and the working of the Holy Spirit, contribute to growth in grace, so that the righteousness that comes from God is preserved and communion with Christ is deepened. When Catholics affirm the "meritorious" character of good works, they wish to say that, according to the biblical witness, a reward in heaven is promised to these works. Their intention is to emphasize the responsibility of persons for their actions, not to contest the character of those works as gifts, or far less to deny that justification always remains the unmerited gift of grace.

39. The concept of a preservation of grace and a growth in grace and faith is also held by Lutherans. They do emphasize that righteousness as acceptance by God and sharing in the righteousness of Christ is always complete. At the same time, they state that there can be growth in its effects in Christian living. When they view the good works of Christians as the fruits and signs of justification and not as one's own "merits," they nevertheless also understand eternal life in accord with the New Testament as unmerited "reward" in the sense of the fulfillment of God's promise to the believer. (See Sources for section 4.7.)

5. The Significance and Scope of the Consensus Reached

40. The understanding of the doctrine of justification set forth in this *Declaration* shows that a consensus in basic truths

of the doctrine of justification exists between Lutherans and Catholics. In light of this consensus the remaining differences of language, theological elaboration, and emphasis in the understanding of justification described in paras. 18 to 39 are acceptable. Therefore the Lutheran and the Catholic explications of justification are in their difference open to one another and do not destroy the consensus regarding the basic truths.

41. Thus the doctrinal condemnations of the sixteenth century, insofar as they relate to the doctrine of justification, appear in a new light: The teaching of the Lutheran churches presented in this *Declaration* does not fall under the condemnations of the Council of Trent. The condemnations in the Lutheran Confessions do not apply to the teaching of the Roman Catholic Church presented in this *Declaration*.

42. Nothing is thereby taken away from the seriousness of the condemnations related to the doctrine of justification. Some were not simply pointless. They remain for us "salutary warnings" to which we must attend in our teaching and practice.[21]

43. Our consensus in basic truths of the doctrine of justification must come to influence the life and teachings of our churches. Here it must prove itself. In this respect, questions of varying importance still need further clarification. These include, among other topics, the relationship between the Word of God and church doctrine, as well as ecclesiology, ecclesial authority, church unity, ministry, the sacraments, and the relation between justification and social ethics. We are convinced that the consensus we have reached offers a solid basis for this clarification. The Lutheran churches and the Roman Catholic Church will con-

---

21. "Condemnations of the Reformation Era," 27.

tinue to strive together to deepen this common understanding of justification and to make it bear fruit in the life and teaching of the churches.

44. We give thanks to the Lord for this decisive step forward on the way to overcoming the division of the church. We ask the Holy Spirit to lead us further toward that visible unity which is Christ's will.

Sources for the
Joint Declaration on the Doctrine of Justification

In parts 3 and 4 of the *Joint Declaration* formulations from different Lutheran-Catholic dialogues are referred to. They include the following documents:

"All under One Christ." Statement on the Augsburg Confession by the Roman Catholic/Lutheran Joint Commission, 1980. In *Growth in Agreement*. Edited by Harding Meyer and Lukas Vischer. New York/Ramsey, N.J., Geneva, 1984, 241-47.

Denzinger-Schönmetzer, *Enchiridion symbolorum* . . . , 32nd to 36th edition (hereafter DS).

Denzinger-Hünermann. *Enchiridion symbolorum* . . . , since the 37th edition (hereafter DH).

"Evaluation of the Pontifical Council for Promoting Christian Unity of the Study 'Lehrverurteilungen — kirchentrennend?' " Vatican, 1992, unpublished document (hereafter PCPCU).

"Justification by Faith." In *Lutherans and Catholics in Dialogue*, VII. Minneapolis, 1985 (hereafter USA).

"Position Paper of the Joint Committee of the United Evangelical Lutheran Church of Germany and the LWF German National Committee regarding the document 'The Condemnations of the Reformation Era. Do They Still Divide?'" In *Lehrverurteilungen im Gespräch*. Göttingen, 1993 (hereafter VELKD).

"The Condemnations of the Reformation Era: Do they Still Divide?" Edited by Karl Lehmann and Wolfhart Pannenberg. Minneapolis, 1990 (hereafter LV:E).

For 3: The Common Understanding of Justification (paras. 17 and 18) (LV:E 68f; VELKD 95)

- ". . . a faith-centered and forensically conceived picture of justification is of major importance for Paul and, in a sense, for the Bible as a whole, although it is by no means the only biblical or Pauline way of representing God's saving work" (USA, no. 146).
- "Catholics as well as Lutherans can acknowledge the need to test the practices, structures, and theologies of the church by the extent to which they help or hinder 'the proclamation of God's free and merciful promises in Christ Jesus, which can be rightly received only through faith' (para. 28)" (USA, no. 153).

Regarding the "fundamental affirmation" (USA, no. 157; cf. 4) it is said:

- "This affirmation, like the Reformation doctrine of justification by faith alone, serves as a criterion for judging all church practices, structures, and traditions precisely because its counterpart is 'Christ alone' *(solus*

Christus). He alone is to be ultimately trusted as the one Mediator through whom God in the Holy Spirit pours out his saving gifts. All of us in this dialogue affirm that all Christian teachings, practices, and offices should so function as to foster 'the obedience of faith' (Rom. 1:5) in God's saving action in Christ Jesus alone through the Holy Spirit, for the salvation of the faithful and the praise and honor of the heavenly Father" (USA, no. 160).

- "For that reason, the doctrine of justification — and, above all, its biblical foundation — will always retain a special function in the church. That function is continually to remind Christians that we sinners live solely from the forgiving love of God, which we merely allow to be bestowed on us, but which we in no way — in however modified a form — 'earn' or are able to tie down to any preconditions or postconditions. The doctrine of justification therefore becomes the touchstone for testing at all times whether a particular interpretation of our relationship to God can claim the name of 'Christian.' At the same time, it becomes the touchstone for the church, for testing at all times whether its proclamation and its praxis correspond to what has been given to it by its Lord" (LV:E 69).
- "An agreement on the fact that the doctrine of justification is significant not only as one doctrinal component within the whole of our church's teaching, but also as the touchstone for testing the whole doctrine and practice of our churches, is — from a Lutheran point of view — fundamental progress in the ecumenical dialogue between our churches. It cannot be welcomed enough" (VELKD 95, 20-26; cf. 157).

- "For Lutherans and Catholics, the doctrine of justification has a different status in the hierarchy of truth; but both sides agree that the doctrine of justification has its specific function in the fact that it is 'the touchstone for testing at all times whether a particular interpretation of our relationship to God can claim the name of "Christian." At the same time it becomes the touchstone for the church, for testing at all times whether its proclamation and its praxis correspond to what has been given to it by its Lord' (LV:E 69). The criteriological significance of the doctrine of justification for sacramentology, ecclesiology and ethical teachings still deserves to be studied further" (PCPCU 96).

For 4.1: Human Powerlessness and Sin in Relation to Justification (paras. 19-21) (LV:E 42ff, 46; VELKD 77-81, 83f)

- "Those in whom sin reigns can do nothing to merit justification, which is the free gift of God's grace. Even the beginnings of justification, for example, repentance, prayer for grace, and desire for forgiveness, must be God's work in us" (USA, no. 156.3).
- "*Both* are concerned to make it clear that . . . human beings cannot . . . cast a sideways glance at their own endeavors. . . . But a response is not a 'work.' The response of faith is itself brought about through the uncoercible word of promise which comes to human beings from outside themselves. There can be '*cooperation*' only in the sense that in faith the heart is involved, when the Word touches it and creates faith" (LV:E 46f).
- "Where, however, Lutheran teaching construes the relation of God to his human creatures in justification with

such emphasis on the divine 'monergism' or the sole efficacy of Christ in such a way that the person's willing acceptance of God's grace — which is itself a gift of God — has no essential role in justification, then the Tridentine canons 4, 5, 6 and 9 still constitute a notable doctrinal difference on justification" (PCPCU 22).

- "The strict emphasis on the passivity of human beings concerning their justification never meant, on the Lutheran side, to contest the full personal participation in believing; rather it meant to exclude any cooperation in the event of justification itself. Justification is the work of Christ alone, the work of grace alone" (VELKD 84, 3-8).

For 4.2: Justification as Forgiveness of Sins and Making Righteous (paras. 22-24) (USA, nos. 98-101; LV:E 47ff; VELKD 84ff; cf. also the quotations for 4.3)

- "By justification we are both declared and made righteous. Justification, therefore, is not a legal fiction. God, in justifying, effects what he promises; he forgives sin and makes us truly righteous" (USA, no. 156, 5).
- "Protestant theology does not overlook what Catholic doctrine stresses: the creative and renewing character of God's love; nor does it maintain . . . God's impotence toward a sin which is 'merely' forgiven in justification but which is not truly abolished in its power to divide the sinner from God" (LV:E 49).
- "The Lutheran doctrine has never understood the 'crediting of Christ's justification' as without effect on the life of the faithful, because Christ's word achieves what it promises. Accordingly the Lutheran doctrine under-

stands grace as God's favor, but nevertheless as effective power . . . 'for where there is forgiveness of sins, there is also life and salvation'" (VELKD 86,15-23).

- "Catholic doctrine does not overlook what Protestant theology stresses: the personal character of grace, and its link with the Word; nor does it maintain . . . grace as an objective 'possession' (even if a conferred possession) on the part of the human being — something over which he can dispose" (LV:E 49).

For 4.3: Justification by Faith and through Grace (paras. 25-27) (USA, nos. 105ff; LV:E 49-53; VELKD 87-90)

- "If we translate from one language to another, then Protestant talk about justification through faith corresponds to Catholic talk about justification through grace; and on the other hand, Protestant doctrine understands substantially under the one word 'faith' what Catholic doctrine (following 1 Cor. 13:13) sums up in the triad of 'faith, hope, and love'" (LV:E 52).
- "We emphasize that faith in the sense of the first commandment always means love to God and hope in him and is expressed in the love to the neighbour" (VELKD 89,8-11).
- "Catholics . . . teach, as do Lutherans, that nothing prior to the free gift of faith merits justification and that all of God's saving gifts come through Christ alone" (USA, no. 105).
- "The Reformers . . . understood faith as the forgiveness and fellowship with Christ effected by the word of promise itself. This is the ground for the new being, through which the flesh is dead to sin and the new man

or woman in Christ has life (*sola fide per Christum*). But even if this faith necessarily makes the human being new, the Christian builds his confidence, not on his own new life, but solely on God's gracious promise. Acceptance in Christ is sufficient, if 'faith' is understood as 'trust in the promise' (*fides promissionis*)" (LV:E 50).

- Cf. The Council of Trent, Session 6, Chap. 7: "Consequently, in the process of justification, together with the forgiveness of sins, a person receives, through Jesus Christ into whom he is grafted, all these infused at the same time: faith, hope and charity" (DH 1530).
- "According to Protestant interpretation, the faith that clings unconditionally to God's promise in Word and Sacrament is sufficient for righteousness before God, so that the renewal of the human being, without which there can be no faith, does not in itself make any contribution to justification" (LV:E 52).
- "As Lutherans we maintain the distinction between justification and sanctification, of faith and works, which however implies no separation" (VELKD 89,6-8).
- "Catholic doctrine knows itself to be at one with the Protestant concern in emphasizing that the renewal of the human being does not 'contribute' to justification, and is certainly not a contribution to which he could make any appeal before God. Nevertheless it feels compelled to stress the renewal of the human being through justifying grace, for the sake of acknowledging God's newly creating power; although this renewal in faith, hope, and love is certainly nothing but a response to God's unfathomable grace" (LV:E 52f).
- "Insofar as the Catholic doctrine stresses that grace is personal and linked with the Word, that renewal . . . is

certainly nothing but a response effected by God's word itself, and that the renewal of the human being does not contribute to justification, and is certainly not a contribution to which a person could make any appeal before God, our objection . . . no longer applies" (VELKD 89,12-21).

For 4.4: The Justified as Sinner (paras. 28-30) (USA, nos. 102ff; LV:E 44ff; VELKD 81ff)

- "For however just and holy, they fall from time to time into the sins that are those of daily existence. What is more, the Spirit's action does not exempt believers from the lifelong struggle against sinful tendencies. Concupiscence and other effects of original and personal sin, according to Catholic doctrine, remain in the justified, who therefore must pray daily to God for forgiveness" (USA, no. 102).
- "The doctrines laid down at Trent and by the Reformers are at one in maintaining that original sin, and also the concupiscence that remains, are in contradiction to God . . . object of the lifelong struggle against sin. . . . [A]fter baptism, concupiscence in the person justified no longer cuts that person off from God; in Tridentine language, it is 'no longer sin in the real sense'; in Lutheran phraseology, it is *peccatum regnatum*, 'controlled sin'" (LV:E 46).
- "The question is how to speak of sin with regard to the justified without limiting the reality of salvation. While Lutherans express this tension with the term 'controlled sin' *(peccatum regnatum)* which expresses the teaching of the Christian as 'being justified and sinner at the same time' *(simul iustus et peccator)*, Roman Catholics think the

34

reality of salvation can only be maintained by denying the sinful character of concupiscence. With regard to this question a considerable rapprochement is reached if LV:E calls the concupiscence that remains in the justified a 'contradiction to God' and thus qualifies it as sin" (VELKD 82,29-39).

For 4.5: Law and Gospel (paras. 31-33)

- According to Pauline teaching this topic concerns the Jewish law as means of salvation. This law was fulfilled and overcome in Christ. This statement and the consequences from it have to be understood on this basis.
- With reference to Canons 19f of the Council of Trent, the VELKD (89,28-36) says as follows: "The ten commandments of course apply to Christians as stated in many places of the confessions. . . . If Canon 20 stresses that a person . . . is bound to keep the commandments of God, this canon does not strike to us; if, however, Canon 20 affirms that faith has salvific power only on condition of keeping the commandments this applies to us. Concerning the reference of the Canon regarding the commandments of the church, there is no difference between us if these commandments are only expressions of the commandments of God; otherwise it would apply to us."
- The last paragraph is related factually to 4.3, but emphasizes the "convicting function" of the law, which is important to Lutheran thinking.

For 4.6: Assurance of Salvation (paras. 34-36) (LV:E 53-56; VELKD 90ff)

- "The question is: How can, and how may, human beings live before God in spite of their weakness, and with that weakness?" (LV:E 53).
- "The foundation and the point of departure [of the Reformers is] . . . the reliability and sufficiency of God's promise, and the power of Christ's death and resurrection; human weakness, and the threat to faith and salvation which that involves" (LV:E 56).
- The Council of Trent also emphasizes that "it is necessary to believe that sins are not forgiven, nor have they ever been forgiven, save freely by the divine mercy on account of Christ"; and that we must not doubt "the mercy of God, the merit of Christ and the power and efficacy of the sacraments; so it is possible for anyone, while he regards himself and his own weakness and lack of dispositions, to be anxious and fearful about his own state of grace" (Council of Trent, Session 6, chapter 9, DH 1534).
- "Luther and his followers go a step farther. They urge that the uncertainty should not merely be endured. We should avert our eyes from it and take seriously, practically, and personally the objective efficacy of the absolution pronounced in the sacrament of penance, which comes 'from outside.' . . . Since Jesus said, 'Whatever you loose on earth shall be loosed in heaven' (Matt. 16:19), the believer . . . would declare Christ to be a liar . . . if he did not rely with a rock-like assurance on the forgiveness of God uttered in the absolution. . . . This reliance can itself be subjectively uncertain — that the assurance of forgiveness is not a security of forgiveness *(securitas)*; but this must not be turned into yet another problem, so to speak: the believer should turn his eyes

36

away from it, and should look only to Christ's word of forgiveness" (LV:E 53f).

- "Today Catholics can appreciate the Reformers' efforts to ground faith in the objective reality of Christ's promise, 'whatsoever you loose on earth . . .' and to focus believers on the specific word of absolution from sins. . . . Luther's original concern to teach people to look away from their experience, and to rely on Christ alone and his word of forgiveness [is not to be condemned]" (PCPCU 24).

- A mutual condemnation regarding the understanding of the assurance of salvation "can even less provide grounds for mutual objection today — particularly if we start from the foundation of a biblically renewed concept of faith. For a person can certainly lose or renounce faith, and self-commitment to God and his word of promise. But if he believes in this sense, he *cannot at the same time* believe that God is unreliable in his word of promise. In this sense it is true today also that — in Luther's words — faith *is* the assurance of salvation" (LV:E 56).

- With reference to the concept of faith of Vatican II, see Dogmatic Constitution on Divine Revelation, no. 5: " 'The obedience of faith' . . . must be given to God who reveals, an obedience by which man entrusts his whole self freely to God, offering 'the full submission of intellect and will to God who reveals,' and freely assenting to the truth revealed by Him."

- "The Lutheran distinction between the certitude (*certitudo*) of faith, which looks alone to Christ, and earthly security (*securitas*), which is based on the human being, has not been dealt with clearly enough in the LV. The question whether a Christian "has believed fully and completely" (LV:E 53) does not arise for the Lutheran understanding, since faith never reflects on itself, but depends completely on God, whose grace is bestowed through word and sacrament, thus from outside *(extra nos)*" (VELKD 92,2-9).

For 4.7: The Good Works of the Justified (paras. 37-39) (LV:E 66ff; VELKD 90ff)

- "But the Council excludes the possibility of earning *grace* — that is, justification — (can. 2: DS 1552) and bases the earning or merit of *eternal life* on the gift of grace itself, through membership in Christ (can. 32: DS 1582). Good works are 'merits' as a *gift*. Although the Reformers attack 'Godless trust' in one's own works, the Council explicitly excludes any notion of a claim or any false security (cap. 16: DS 1548f). It is evident . . . that the Council wishes to establish a link with Augustine, who introduced the concept of merit, in order to express the responsibility of human beings, in spite of the 'bestowed' character of good works" (LV:E 66).
- If we understand the language of "cause" in Canon 24 in more personal terms, as it is done in chapter 16 of the Decree on Justification, where the idea of communion with Christ is foundational, then we can describe the Catholic doctrine on merit as it is done in the first sentence of the second paragraph of 4.7: growth in grace, perseverance in righteousness received from God and a deeper communion with Christ.
- "Many antitheses could be overcome if the misleading word 'merit' were simply to be viewed and thought

about in connection with the true sense of the biblical term 'wage' or reward" (LV:E 67).

- "The Lutheran confessions stress that the justified person is responsible not to lose the grace received but to live in it. . . . Thus the confessions can speak of a preservation of grace and a growth in it. If righteousness in Canon 24 is understood in the sense that it affects human beings, then it does not strike us. But if 'righteousness' in Canon 24 refers to the Christian's acceptance by God, it does strike us; for this righteousness is always perfect; compared with it the works of Christians are only 'fruits' and 'signs'" (VELKD 94,2-14).

- "Concerning Canon 26, we refer to the Apology, where eternal life is described as reward: '. . . We grant that eternal life is a reward because it is something that is owed — not because of our merits but because of the promise'" (VELKD 94,20-24).

OFFICIAL COMMON STATEMENT

*by the Lutheran World Federation
and the Catholic Church*

1. On the basis of the agreements reached in the *Joint Declaration on the Doctrine of Justification (JD)*, the Lutheran World Federation and the Catholic Church declare together: "The understanding of the doctrine of justification set forth in this *Declaration* shows that a consensus in basic truths of the doctrine of justification exists between Lutherans and Catholics" (*JD* no. 40). On the basis of this consensus the Lutheran World Federation and the Catholic Church declare together: "The teaching of the Lutheran Churches presented in this *Declaration* does not fall under the condemnations of the Council of Trent. The condemnations in the Lutheran Confessions do not apply to the teaching of the Roman Catholic Church presented in this *Declaration*" (*JD* no. 41).

2. With reference to the Resolution on the Joint Declaration by the Council of the Lutheran World Federation of 16 June 1998 and the response to the Joint Declaration by the Catholic Church of 25 June 1998 and to the questions raised by both of them, the annexed statement (called "Annex") further substantiates the consensus reached in the *Joint Declaration;* thus it becomes clear that the earlier mutual doctrinal condemnations do not apply to the teaching of the dialogue partners as presented in the *Joint Declaration*.

3. The two partners in dialogue are committed to continued and deepened study of the biblical foundations of the doctrine of justification. They will also seek further common understanding of the doctrine of justification, also beyond what is dealt with in the *Joint Declaration* and the annexed substantiating statement. Based on the consensus reached, continued dialogue is required specifically on the issues mentioned especially in the *Joint Declaration* itself (JD no. 43) as requiring further clarification in order to reach full church communion, a unity in diversity, in which remaining differences would be "reconciled" and no longer have a divisive force. Lutherans and Catholics will continue their efforts ecumenically in their common witness to interpret the message of justification in language relevant for human beings today, and with reference both to individual and social concerns of our times.

By this act of signing
The Catholic Church and The Lutheran World Federation
confirm
the Joint Declaration on the Doctrine of Justification
in its entirety.

ANNEX TO THE OFFICIAL
COMMON STATEMENT

1. The following elucidations underline the consensus reached in the *Joint Declaration on the Doctrine of Justification (JD)* regarding basic truths of justification; thus it becomes clear that the mutual condemnations of former times do not apply to the Catholic and Lutheran doctrines of justification as they are presented in the *Joint Declaration.*

2. "Together we confess: By grace alone, in faith in Christ's saving work and not because of any merit on our part, we are accepted by God and receive the Holy Spirit, who renews our hearts while equipping and calling us to good works" (*JD* no. 15).

   A "We confess together that God forgives sin by grace and at the same time frees human beings from sin's enslaving power . . ." (*JD* no. 22). Justification is forgiveness of sins and being made righteous, through which God "imparts the gift of new life in Christ" (*JD* no. 22). "Since we are justified by faith we have peace with God" (Rom 5:1). We are "called children of God; and that is what we are" (1 Jn 3:1). We are truly and inwardly renewed by the action of the Holy Spirit, remaining always dependent on his work in us. "So if anyone is in Christ, there is a new creation: everything old has passed away; see, everything has become new!" (2 Cor 5:17). The justified do not remain sinners in this sense.

Yet we would be wrong were we to say that we are without sin (1 Jn 1:8-10; cf. *JD* no. 28). "(A)ll of us make many mistakes" (Jas 3:2). "Who is aware of his unwitting sins? Cleanse me of many secret faults" (Ps. 19:12). And when we pray, we can only say, like the tax collector, "God, be merciful to me, a sinner" (Lk 18:13). This is expressed in a variety of ways in our liturgies. Together we hear the exhortation "Therefore, do not let sin exercise dominion in your mortal bodies, to make you obey their passions" (Rom 6:12). This recalls to us the persisting danger that comes from the power of sin and its action in Christians. To this extent, Lutherans and Catholics can together understand the Christian as *simul justus et peccator,* despite their different approaches to this subject as expressed in *JD* nos. 29-30.

B   The concept of "concupiscence" is used in different senses on the Catholic and Lutheran sides. In the Lutheran Confessional writings "concupiscence" is understood as the self-seeking desire of the human being, which in light of the law, spiritually understood, is regarded as sin. In the Catholic understanding concupiscence is an inclination, remaining in human beings even after baptism, which comes from sin and presses toward sin. Despite the differences involved here, it can be recognized from a Lutheran perspective that desire can become the opening through which sin attacks. Due to the power of sin the entire human being carries the tendency to oppose God. This tendency, according to both the Lutheran and the Catholic conception, "does not correspond to God's original design for humanity" (*JD* no. 30). Sin has a personal character and, as such, leads to separation from God. It is the selfish desire of the old person and the lack of trust and love toward God.

The reality of salvation in baptism and the peril from the power of sin can be expressed in such a way that, on the one hand, the forgiveness of sins and renewal of humanity in Christ by baptism are emphasized and, on the other hand, it can be seen that the justified also "are continuously exposed to the power of sin still pressing its attacks (cf. Rom 6:12-14) and are not exempt from a lifelong struggle against the contradiction to God . . ." (*JD* no. 28).

C Justification takes place "by grace alone" (*JD* nos. 15 and 16), by faith alone; the person is justified "apart from works" (Rom 3:28; cf. *JD* no. 25). "Grace creates faith not only when faith begins in a person but as long as faith lasts" (Thomas Aquinas, *STh* II/II 4, 4 ad 3). The working of God's grace does not exclude human action: God effects everything, the willing and the achievement, therefore, we are called to strive (cf. Phil 2:12ff). "As soon as the Holy Spirit has initiated his work of regeneration and renewal in us through the Word and the holy sacraments, it is certain that we can and must cooperate by the power of the Holy Spirit . . ." (The Formula of Concord [FC], SD II,64f; BSLK 897,37ff).

D Grace as fellowship of the justified with God in faith, hope, and love is always received from the salvific and creative work of God (cf. *JD* no. 27). But it is nevertheless the responsibility of the justified not to waste this grace but to live in it. The exhortation to do good works is the exhortation to practice the faith (cf. BSLK

45

197,45). The good works of the justified "should be done in order to confirm their call, that is, lest they fall from their call by sinning again" (Apol. XX,13, BSLK 316,18-24; with reference to 2 Pet. 1:10. Cf. also FC SD IV,33; BSLK 948,9-23). In this sense Lutherans and Catholics can understand together what is said about the "preservation of grace" in *JD* nos. 38 and 39. Certainly, "whatever in the justified precedes or follows the free gift of faith is neither the basis of justification nor merits it" (*JD* no. 25).

E   By justification we are unconditionally brought into communion with God. This includes the promise of eternal life; "(I)f we have been united with him in a death like his, we will certainly be united with him in a resurrection like his" (Rom 6:5; cf. Jn 3:36; Rom 8:17). In the final judgment, the justified will be judged also on their works (cf. Mt 16:27; 25:31-46; Rom 2:16; 14:12; 1 Cor 3:8; 2 Cor 5:10, etc.). We face a judgment in which God's gracious sentence will approve anything in our life and action that corresponds to his will. However, everything in our life that is wrong will be uncovered and will not enter eternal life. The Formula of Concord also states: "It is God's will and express command that believers should do good works, which the Holy Spirit works in them, and God is willing to be pleased with them for Christ's sake and he promises to reward them gloriously in this and in the future life" (FC SD IV,38). Any reward is a reward of grace, on which we have no claim.

3.   The doctrine of justification is that measure or touchstone for the Christian faith. No teaching may contradict this criterion. In this sense, the doctrine of justification is

an "indispensable criterion that constantly serves to orient all the teaching and practice of our churches to Christ" (*JD* no. 18). As such, it has its truth and specific meaning within the overall context of the church's fundamental Trinitarian confession of faith. We "share the goal of confessing Christ in all things, who alone is to be trusted above all things as the one Mediator (1 Tim 2:5f) through whom God in the Holy Spirit gives himself and pours out his renewing gifts" (*JD* no. 18).

4. The Response of the Catholic Church does not intend to put in question the authority of Lutheran Synods or of the Lutheran World Federation. The Catholic Church and the Lutheran World Federation began the dialogue and have taken it forward as partners with equal rights (*par cum pari*). Notwithstanding different conceptions of authority in the church, each partner respects the other partner's ordered process of reaching doctrinal decisions.